MECHANICS' INSTITUTE
⸙ MECHANICS' ⸙
MERCANTILE LIBRARY

DRESSAGE
Begin the Right Way

MECHANICS' INSTITUTE

DRESSAGE
Begin the Right Way

LOCKIE RICHARDS

Photography by
Alix Coleman

DAVID & CHARLES
NEWTON ABBOT   LONDON
NORTH POMFRET (VT)   VANCOUVER

ISBN 0 7153 6926 1
Library of Congress Catalog Card Number 75-6

© Lockie Richards 1975

All rights reserved. No part of this publication may be reproduced, stored in a retrieval system, or transmitted, in any form or by any means, electronic, mechanical, photocopying, recording or otherwise, without the prior permission of David & Charles (Holdings) Limited

Set in 12 on 13 point Bembo
and printed in Great Britain
by Redwood Burn Ltd, Trowbridge & Esher
for David & Charles (Holdings) Limited
South Devon House Newton Abbot Devon

Published in the United States of America
by David & Charles Inc North Pomfret Vermont 05053 USA

Published in Canada by Douglas David & Charles Limited
132 Philip Avenue North Vancouver BC

798.2
R51

Contents

276100

Preface

I have tried in this book to make dressage a word that is not surrounded by mystery but one that the average horseman can use and not be afraid that he will be classified as a prima donna. Dressage is of course practised, in different forms, by many who do not accept or even recognise the word. I hope that I can open the door for some of these people and also make the basic principles clear and easy to follow for the average horseman.

As you will have gathered already, the book is not written for the experts. They may see some points in a different light; every instructor explains and uses a slightly different terminology. The key word in an explanation may open up new horizons for one pupil and, on the other hand, mean absolutely nothing to another. One cannot learn to ride or train from a book alone. The most important point is to understand the theory and principles and to learn from the horse in applying them. Many riders are so busy applying too many aids that they completely forget to feel how the horse responds. I hope that I have succeeded in giving riders some idea of what they should expect to feel and how to learn from their horses.

There are many people who have been put off dressage because they do not have the figure of a Grecian god or goddess, or possess a horse with perfect conformation. It must be understood that anyone, with patience and the ambition to improve their horse, can understand and execute basic dressage.

I would like to express my thanks to my parents for encouraging me to pursue a career with horses. I would also like to thank Miss Winifred Lysnar for helping me to make the decision to become an instructor.

From every one of my instructors, pupils and their horses, I have learnt something of lasting value. I consider myself most fortunate in having had the opportunity to work with Mr Robert Hall and Oberbereiter Franz Rockowansky.

I am most grateful also to Miss Alix Coleman for the fine photography and the many hours she spent in capturing the right moments and to my wife for her patience and hours of typing.

L.R.

Chapter 1

The Aims of Training

The word 'dressage' means the training of a horse to improve his natural balance and movement. Many people are of the erroneous opinion that the term dressage refers to a horse when he is always in a form of collection or performing high-school movements. Usually they have reached this conclusion as a result of watching exhibitions of highly trained horses, which have of course received all the necessary training years before but are still capable of showing all the basic movements. Classical dressage means that the horse is trained by a systematic sequence of exercises to perform all the natural movements which he would normally do on his own when at liberty. Circus dressage usually includes these natural movements plus a number of unnatural movements or tricks. We are concerned here only with classical dressage.

The methods of training have remained basically the same since the first book on riding was written by Xenophon in about 400 BC. This is logical when you consider that by and large the physical form of both man and horse has not changed much since then. The first important school on record was founded at Naples, with the nobleman Federigo Grisone as riding master. Grisone's best pupil was Pignatelli, who in turn trained the Frenchman Pluvinel who was employed by Louis XIII as his court riding master.

Pluvinel's methods were less forceful than those of his teacher and it took some time for them to be generally accepted. In this same period, in the middle of the seventeenth century, the Duke of Newcastle was very much interested in the art of 'high school'. His methods were widespread in England but were later rejected, as were those of Pignatelli.

9

In 1733 the most famous riding master of France, F. R. dè la Guériniere, wrote a book. This was based on simple facts and details, which influenced the art for a long time. In fact, to this day they are the doctrine followed at the Spanish Riding School of Vienna. As far back as 1572 the name of Spanish Riding Stable was known and in 1735 the school opened at its present site. The cavalry schools from all over Europe sent their officers to train there, and since then their methods have been accepted in most countries.

Every race has certain characteristics that influence, intentionally or not, their interpretation and execution of dressage. The national breed of horse which is used also varies in temperament. The conformation of certain breeds makes it possible for them to perform some movements more graciously than others. The West Germans perform very accurate, active, precise and sometimes stilted tests. The Russians are more artistic with flowing, supple and expressive performances. Generally the Swiss and riders from the Scandinavian countries give the impression of casualness with very willing and happy horses. The French are inclined to brilliance and a flamboyant expression. The English are very correct with strong ideals on classical form. The East Germans produce classical and quietly serene horses and riders.

The aim in training should be to produce an obedient, supple and happy horse; one who wants to work on his own and carry himself with no force and as little drive from the rider as possible. In other words, the rider should do as little as possible but as much as is necessary. This may vary from day to day. Horses, like people, are susceptible to changes of mood and to changes of physical ability: what you may only have to suggest to your horse today, you may well have to ask or even demand tomorrow. The basic principles of training remain the same, no matter what the horse will specialise in later on. For the hunter, the pleasure horse, the event horse, the show jumper and the competition dressage horse, all the preliminary requirements and exercises are the same.

The horse, if trained correctly, will go forward willingly in the open, looking where he is going and using his own initiative as to where to put his feet, yet willing to listen to the rider's slightest command. If a horse is trained by a completely dominating method, whereby the rider asks constantly for the amount of impulsion, rhythm and length of stride, problems will arise in as far as hunting, eventing and show-jumping go. Even the most talented of riders can make a mistake and, if the horse has not been allowed to think for himself and carry himself, disaster may follow.

The important combination to remember is that the rider should physically become part of the horse and the horse in turn should mentally reciprocate and become part of the rider. This is not always easy to achieve. Some riders find it very difficult mentally to allow themselves physically to go with the horse, especially when the horse is not mentally going with them. Relaxation and confidence help to achieve this. When forming a partnership, one party has to give first. If the rider does this by being relaxed and going with the horse, the horse will surely follow. The rider needs to understand his horse and therefore ride him mentally and not physically. I am not saying that certain physical aids and influences are never to be used, but invariably it is a case of too much brawn and not enough brain. The impression given by a horse and rider should be that they are as one, and attention should not be brought to any one particular part of the combination. The outward effect should be of poise, elegance and softness, of a flowing movement emanating from behind.

Chapter 2

The Ideal Horse and Rider

THE HORSE

As I mentioned earlier, it is possible to train practically any horse, whether he has good conformation or not. There is the ideal horse but this depends to a large extent on the rider: a horse which is ideal in size and temperament for one rider is not necessarily so for another.

When choosing a horse to train for dressage it is advisable to study his natural movement by watching him when at liberty or on the lunge without a saddle or bridle. It is very important that the horse should move in one piece and that your attention

Plate 1   Observe potential competitor horse at liberty to note especially self carriage and movement

Plate 2

is not directed to a pretty head or flashing front legs. It is wise
to take particular notice of the engagement of his hind legs from
both the side and the back. The movement should be straight
and true with all joints being used equally. If the horse is beautiful
when standing still, he must be equally beautiful and co-ordinated
when in movement (see plate 1). It is helpful if the horse carries
himself in a horizontal position, but if he is a little on the forehand
as many young horses are, remember that this can be corrected
with training. When the horse carries himself correctly in the
trot, he should track with the mark of the hind foot covering
or overreaching the mark made by the front foot. In the walk, the
hind hoof print should come well over the front hoof print. If the
horse has a long back this may not be possible, but ideally it is
preferred. Some riders have a naturally good eye for a well-
balanced horse who uses the whole of his body when moving.
Others may need the opinion of another party, preferably their
instructor.

Most horses in dressage competition are of a thoroughbred

Plate 3

Plate 4

type. Horses with high or round action are now generally considered more suitable for exhibition purposes as they find it easier to perform collected movements, piaffe and passage. The majority of top class horses are between 16 and 17 hands high. Three different types can be seen in plates 2–4: a thoroughbred of good conformation with attractive markings; a fine type of Hanoverian; and the heavier Westphalian. The colour of the horse is a matter of personal preference but two white hind socks or four white socks and white on the face are definitely eye-catching.

The temperament of the horse is really more important than the conformation. It is generally easier to change the physique of a horse with training than to alter his temperament. To a certain extent it is possible to tell from a horse's eye and expression if he is quiet and generous. The horse must be willing to listen to the rider and accept the aids without question. Stallions are much favoured for dressage work as they are quick to learn and take discipline very well. Mares on the other hand tend to be more changeable in temperament and therefore not always consistent but invariably they are very sensitive. Geldings are normally the most consistent in performance but are not always as brilliant as a stallion or mare. For competition dressage a gelding would be the most desirable, except for a stallion or mare with an exceptional disposition.

THE RIDER

Any rider can work in dressage, providing he has the ambition or interest. A person who is long and lean has fewer problems and looks well on a horse. The rider with a good length of thigh and not too long a back can sit deep in the saddle and keep his balance more easily. One who is too long from the hips to the bottom rib often has problems in co-ordinating the upper with the lower body – a bit like the horse with a long back. Riders, like horses, can also be trained to alter their form. Those with thick thighs or over-muscular calves can change them with continuous exercise. The most important attributes for a dressage rider are balance, poise and a good sense of rhythm. These qualities may come naturally, but you can be trained to acquire them.

Like the horse, the temperament of the serious dressage rider is important. He must be able to take the discipline and, above all, be patient. A dressage horse, like a gymnast or ballet dancer, needs to be worked every day to develop, strengthen and keep his body supple. The rider must understand this and be willing to make the necessary sacrifices. A rider must know exactly the goals he hopes to achieve and also be aware of his own physical and temperament problems so that the horse does not suffer as a result of them. He must be prepared to let himself physically become part of the horse and must also learn to think as the horse thinks and then be able to mentally tune in to him.

Chapter 3

Position of the Rider

I am starting with the position of the rider, because until he can sit in a way which enables him to be relaxed and supple, he has little hope of influencing the horse. The most satisfactory way to teach position with either an experienced or inexperienced rider is on the lunge.

To mount the rider takes the reins and whip in the left hand with just enough contact to check the horse in case he should think of moving. The left hand should be placed by the wither. He takes the stirrup with the right hand and gives it a half turn in a clockwise direction so that, when he is mounted, the stirrup leather will be correctly placed. Facing the horse's quarters, he places the left foot right home in the stirrup with the toe down by the girth, and hops around to face across the waist of the saddle. With the right hand, he takes hold of the pommel, or across the waist of the saddle, and springs to a standing position, at the same time straightening the left arm. He swings the right leg over and allows his seat to drop lightly into the saddle. Placing the foot in the right stirrup he is now ready for work.

The horse should be lunged for a minute or two to get his back loosened up and to make sure that the side reins are the required length. (For the correct lungeing procedure see page 27.) The aim with an inexperienced rider is to obtain a good working position in which he feels comfortable and is able to co-ordinate his movement with that of the horse. It is helpful to use a saddle with a deep seat like the one in the photograph and also in plate 2, page 13.

The rider's seat should be in the centre of the saddle, this

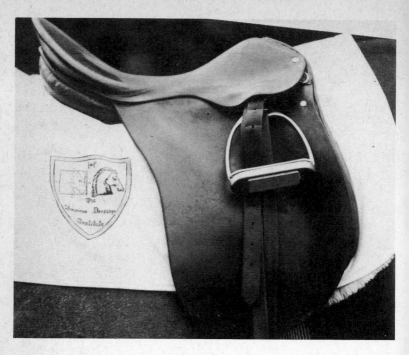

Plate 5

being the deepest part and he should feel his seat bones like two little sleds. The upper body should be upright with the back in a natural position—that is, slightly arched, definitely not collapsed in the middle, or stiff or rigid. The term 'braced back' is usually misinterpreted and the result is a hollow stiff back. The rider's back is very important in respect of maintaining balance and being able to co-ordinate leg and hand aids. The head must be up with a long neck above square shoulders. The rider should look to the front and in the direction of the movement. He should give the impression that he is observing himself in a mirror from a distance. The shoulders should be back and dropped down. If they are dropped forward, the back will tend to become round making it very difficult for him to keep his balance. The tendency usually is to lift the shoulders and therefore stiffen the arms. The arm should hang loosely from the shoulder with the elbow in the vicinity of the hip. The elbow is bent, allowing a straight line to form from the elbow, through

Plate 6   Kie Johnson, USA, on Fleury

Plate 7   H. Blocker, Germany, on Albrant

Plate 8   Sidley Payne on the Portuguese-bred Felix *and Kie Johnson on* Fleury

the forearm hand and rein to the horse's mouth. The hands are held in a natural position; closed, as though holding a small bird, with the left thumb pointing towards the horse's right ear and the right thumb towards the horse's left ear. The reins are held between the third and the little finger and past the first knuckle. The leg is dropped down with the knee slightly bent. The thigh contact should be on the inside to allow a close contact with the horse. The lower leg from the knee down, is in contact with the horse's side. Again, the inside or thinner part of the calf is in contact. The foot is at a natural angle and, as near as possible, parallel to the horse's side. The heel is down with the ball of the foot on the stirrup, the weight evenly distributed as when standing on the ground; not with more weight on the inside or big toe as this tends to take the leg away from the horse's side. When the heel is down, the calf muscles become tight enabling the horse to feel the leg aids more clearly. But it should not be forced down as this tends to stiffen the knee and tighten the thigh and seat muscles. It also tends to force the seat back in the saddle causing discomfort to the horse, who will then stiffen his back. This in turn causes discomfort to the rider, who will then tend to collapse his back and create a balance problem for the horse. The correction for getting the heel down comes by placing the seat bones in the centre of the saddle, with a relaxed thigh.

From the side, the rider should form a straight line from the ear to the shoulder, hip and heel. From the front, the rider should have his head directly over the horse's spine with both his shoulders at the same height, both legs the same length and both feet at the same angle. The rider will now have an even distribution of weight on both seat bones. Plates 6–8 show good positions.

Work on the lunge is commenced at the walk. I like to start at the head and work down. The first exercise is for the rider to circle the head loosely, dropping it down in front and rolling it around to one shoulder and then back and around to the other shoulder. All exercises are done in both directions. I like to ask the rider which direction he finds the easiest. This way he remembers and can work on it at home in front of a mirror. Next the head, dropping from one shoulder to the other. This loosens the vital vertebrae that gives freedom to the whole spine.

These exercises are followed with shoulder circling, first back and then forward, one shoulder at a time and then both together, but only the shoulder – no arm movement. This is a very beneficial exercise for relaxation. Remember also that the jaw is one of the first things that we clamp when stiff or tense. To yawn a few times or even sing helps to keep it relaxed. A number of show-jumping riders have used chewing gum to help them, but this is of course extremely dangerous when riding.

Arms circling backwards alternately like a windmill, and then both together, will loosen tight shoulder muscles that men especially suffer from, and open the chest. Make sure that when these exercises are performed, only the particular limb being used is moving. Watch that the legs do not try and follow the arm movements. With both hands straight out in front, the arms are swung back at shoulder height and both hands clapped behind the back. Swinging both arms together from side to side loosens the waist. A vital exercise for the development and co-ordination of seat, leg and hand aids is to lift the chest with a feeling of being pulled up by a string from the ceiling. It creates the effect of having a higher, wider chest, as when you take a long deep breath, and separates the lower ribs from the hips, allowing independent movement of the seat.

To help find the correct upright position, the rider should round his back and drop his head and then go to the reverse position with his back hollow and his head up. He completes the exercise with a correctly aligned shoulder and hip.

Leg exercises should start with stretching the leg out sideways and allowing it to come back with the muscles or excess thigh to the back; a beneficial exercise for the ladies with large thighs. The legs can be swung out alternately and then both together, making sure that both hips remain the same height and that the shoulder on the same side does not collapse. Particular attention must be paid to the correctness of the upper body. This is more important than how far out the legs can be moved.

The rider can now combine leg and arm exercises to help with co-ordination. He circles the arm up and backwards and at the same time, swings the lower leg back so that the heel is touched with the hand. This stretches the stomach muscles, pushes the hips forward, and lengthens the thigh. Next, he swings his arms and lower legs in a marching movement. Usually the tendency is to move the legs in the same direction as the hands instead of the opposite. If this exercise is not mastered it means that should he apply a leg aid, the hand on the same side is also likely to move, contradicting the leg aid.

Once these exercises are accomplished at the walk, they are then done at the trot. I usually make the rider do a little work in rising trot (with stirrups) making sure that his lower leg is completely independent of the upper leg. Whether the rider is rising or sitting the lower leg should not move in excess of the necessary absorbing movement of the knee and ankle. A good test to find out whether or not the lower leg is correct is to have the rider come to the top of his rising and stay there, by balance, if possible, or holding the mane but not on the horse's mouth. If he can stay up quite easily, then you can be sure that his lower leg is correct, providing that when he sits, he bends the knee and does not shoot the leg forward. In the rising trot, the rider should make sure that he is relaxed and that the horse throws him up and that he allows himself to come down quietly. He must not push himself up or drop down heavily behind the movement. If he has a problem because of a stiff or gripping knee and thigh with the lower leg shooting forward, he will need to relax the thigh and let the knee and ankle bend.

We now work in sitting trot without stirrups. At this point the rider should be thinking of going with the rhythm of the horse and being absolutely relaxed. When making corrections of position, he may hold the pommel and pull his seat down and hips forward, at the same time sitting tall and lengthening the thigh. Sit up and sit down. This correction is very important as when the rider feels at all unbalanced, ie when the horse becomes unbalanced or before transitions and changes of direction, he must sit tall, drop the seat and close the leg. I do not like to use the word 'grip' as the natural tendency is to grip upwards, thus shortening the leg and pushing the seat back, causing the upper body to fall forward. This shifting of weight adds another problem for the horse. All the rider needs to do is relax his seat and thigh muscles and allow the horse to come up to his seat bones, and at that moment close the leg and then relax it. Thus, the checking of the position is a down and an around movement.

When the rider is quite at ease, we work on transitions on the lunge without holding the saddle. At this point we can start working in the canter. Arms swinging in a marching movement in time with the canter, helps the rider to sit relaxed and go with his horse. If the rider can sit and do nothing in the canter this is all we should ask. Many riders try too hard to go with the movement and slide the seat or swing the upper body, again causing a problem for the horse. The saying 'once you can do nothing, then you can do something' should be thought about. It is easy to do a lot, but not so easy to do a very little.

Once the rider becomes proficient on the lunge without the reins, we let him take them, checking to see that he maintains an even contact by watching the bit in the horse's mouth. If it is pulled through to one side, the contact will usually be uneven. If the seat is correct and is independent of the legs and hands, the contact will remain even during the transitions.

Everyday before he rides, the conscientious rider will do all the necessary exercises that apply to his particular stiffness. In this way the horse at least has a chance, by starting off with a relaxed and supple rider. The horse can only become balanced and supple if the rider is likewise. A stiff or tense rider will cause the horse to be stiff, even if he was supple to start with. A constant check has to be kept on position as the leg that once was loose may now be still while the other leg may have become loose. The rider can not arrive at the perfect position and then forget about it, the leading riders have trainers constantly watching and correcting little faults which may affect the horse's performance.

The aim is to ride with a long leg and deep seat. With the leg long we have a close contact with the horse and can feel his movement more easily. We can also learn to be as sensitive with our legs as with our hands and also to feel with the legs. It depends to a certain extent on the width of the horse and his stage of training as to the length of the stirrup leathers. The important point is to ride only as long as is possible, while still being effective. A rough guide is when the foot is out of the stirrup, the bottom of the iron should come just below the ankle bone.

On the lunge the points to watch are that the rider does not drop the inside shoulder and collapse the inside hip, thus shortening the inside leg. Be careful that his outside leg does not come away with his toe out. This is difficult to see from the inside of the circle and it pays to have someone standing on the outside occasionally. The other point is to make sure that his outside shoulder is very slightly in advance of his inside one. The rider's weight will now automatically come more onto his inside seat bone. Again, I try not to emphasise putting the weight on the inside as most riders usually lean to the inside in trying to do so.

If you have a problem of stiffness in any movement with your horse, do not be afraid to get on the lunge and check out the evenness and co-ordination of yourself before trying to correct the horse. The saying 'It is always the rider's fault' is in most cases true. But you should not get a complex about always being at fault; sometimes the horse needs his mental attitude changed or a physical problem corrected.

Chapter 4

Training the Young Horse

HANDLING

The training of a young horse begins from the moment we catch
him in the field. He is taught to stand and even at this stage, we can
start by getting him to stand squarely on all four feet (see plate 9).
Next we accustom him to the whip, which he should respect but
not be afraid of. Let him smell it and press it on his lips. The
horse's sense of smell and touch by the lips are important to him.
When we teach him to lead, he should come up by our side and
not trail behind like a dog. If he hangs back, give him a touch just
behind his girth with the whip. We use the whip behind our back
and keep looking forward, otherwise the horse may be inclined
to run back. The young horse should lead from both sides and
allow himself to be generally handled, groomed, and have his feet
picked up from both sides.

LUNGEING

When the young horse is three years old and if he is sufficiently
developed, we can start to lunge him. With a lungeing cavesson,
lunge rein, long whip, and brushing boots on in front to protect
him in case he should knock his fetlocks, take him and an assistant
to an enclosed area. If there is no small paddock or yard use the
corner of a field, where at least it will be helpful to have two sides.
Lead the horse on a circle of about 15m (about 50ft) diameter with
the assistant holding the cavesson lightly on the off side. Gradually walk away from the horse letting out the lunge line until he
is on the circle, and then stand still allowing the assistant to lead
him on the outside. Form a triangle by facing the horse's middle,

Plate 9   Denny Emerson, USA, and Victor Dakin practise a square halt

with the lunge rein forming a straight line from your elbow to the
horse's nose, and the whip pointing towards his hock (see plate
10). Your heel should keep pivoting, ie if you are lungeing in an
anti-clockwise direction, the left heel should remain in the one
spot. You will then acquire a correct circle and the horse will
travel in one track thus becoming balanced more easily.

Plate 10

Right from the beginning the horse is taught to accept a contact of the hand to his nose through the lunge rein, equivalent to the contact with his mouth, through the rein and bit later on. We also teach him to accept the whip aid, which activates the hind legs as will the rider's legs later on in his training.

Once the horse is walking quietly on both reins and listening to the voice aids of 'walk on', 'halt', 'whoa' or 'ho', we teach him to trot with the assistant jogging by his side. Make sure that the horse is rewarded when he halts by either patting him all over or giving him sugar, a carrot, or whatever he likes. Try to use the voice quietly, as a horse has very sensitive hearing. The commands should be given with an expression and in the tone of how you would like the horse to respond, ie a quick brisk command for a quick brisk response, a slow drawn out one for a quiet progressive transition down.

The assistant can now let go of the cavesson and gradually walk

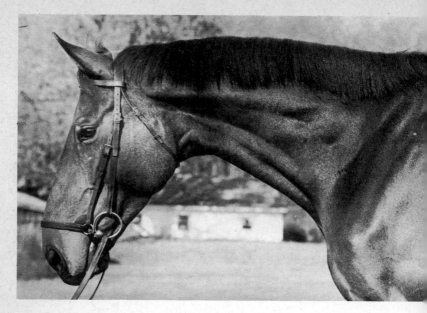

Plate 11   Loose-ring snaffle with dropped noseband

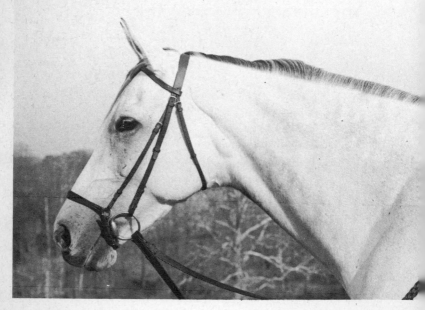

Plate 12   Egg-butt snaffle

away, taking care that there is no wall or fence on his other side, so that if the horse should take fright and leap forward or sideways or kick out, he has a better chance of moving out of the way. We would repeat the same procedure for several days and try to dispense with the assistant. Remember, only lunge for 15–20 minutes, working on a circle is extremely tiring and a strain on muscles and joints that are unaccustomed to working hard. By this time you will know in which direction the horse prefers to travel. If his spine is bent to the left, which you can see from behind as his tail will curve in that direction, he will prefer to travel the same way. It is wise always to do what is easiest for the horse first, and to work on the difficult side later. This way he feels comfortable physically and will relax, so that any stiffness felt will be lessened when working on his more difficult side. We follow this theory all through his training, helping the horse by presenting all new exercises to him in a manner that he will find acceptable.

Gradually the lungeing time is extended to 30 minutes or longer and the horse is introduced to wearing a thick single-jointed snaffle (see plates 11–12, showing the thick loose-ring snaffle and egg-butt snaffle with drop nose-bands). It is advisable to use a drop nose-band to prevent the horse from opening his mouth and acquiring the habit of evading the bit. The saddle should be put on in the stable with the stirrups up, before lungeing him with it on. Next we put on loose side reins attached to the first girth or billet strap so that they will not drop down too low. The side reins should both be the same length. They are gradually taken up shorter over a period of weeks until the horse is stretching onto a contact (see plate 13, lungeing equipment). When adjusting the cavesson, make sure that the strap which goes around the jowl is really tight so that should the horse pull when the lunge line is attached to the centre ring, the jowl strap will not rub on his eye causing him to pull out even more because of the discomfort. The lower or cavesson strap should also be very firm . . . to prevent it from moving and rubbing the horse. The jowl strap goes on the outside of the bridle while the cavesson strap should go underneath (see plate 13).

Plate 13

When the horse is working correctly on the lunge, the hind legs follow the tracks of the front legs. When the inside hind, which has to take more of the weight and therefore drive more, is working well foreward, the horse will bend from behind all the way through his spine. The inside side rein may now appear a little loose while the horse is bent to the inside (see plate 10, page 29). If you try to obtain the bend by shortening the inside side rein, only the neck bends and the horse usually pushes his shoulder out or swings his hind-quarters away.

BACKING

Once the horse is really obedient to the voice aids and is sufficiently balanced and strong enough, we teach him to accept a rider. As is normal in training, all new exercises are introduced at the end of the day's work. We start by legging the assistant up, so that he can lay across the saddle. It is not usually the weight but the sight of an object above that frightens a horse. His natural instinct tells him to run from fear of anything that is about to pounce on him from above. When he has become accustomed to the rider across the saddle, we can walk him a few steps. Gradually with soothing words and many rewards, the rider can slowly put his leg over and sit upright, taking both stirrups.

The following day we repeat the exercise and now walk with the rider mounted. Gradually we let him out on the lunge and proceed to lunge him normally. The rider must be very relaxed as nothing will upset the horse quicker than someone sitting on him gripping wildly and waiting to be bucked off. The rider should hold the pommel of the saddle or a neck strap and just simply go with the horse, rising to the trot and sitting quietly during the transitions. When the horse is quite happy, the rider should use simple leg aids ie quiet little vibrations with the upper, inner calf at the same time as the voice aids are given. The next step is to hold the reins. As a preliminary exercise, I like to have a set of reins attached to the side rings on the lungeing cavesson, later holding the reins attached to the bit.

We can now walk the horse around an enclosed area, gradually detaching the lunge rein and walking away as the assistant did beforehand. The rider can soon walk and trot and change the rein diagonally across the school. If you do not have an enclosed area, then either have someone on a quiet horse to lead the young horse or make him follow around in a large circle. When the horse is confident and listening to quiet aids to go forward and the voice aid for transitions down, he may be hacked out with a quiet companion.

Try in the beginning stages to get the young horse used to streams, up and down hills, bridges, and any other things that he may not be accustomed to, while he still has a leader. In the next year he should be worked lightly or if there is good pasture on hill country he should be turned out to develop further. Some breeds develop very late and it is best if the horse has nearly fully developed before serious training begins. If the horse has to be stabled or has only limited exercise areas, he is better off worked quietly, lunged occasionally, and turned out when possible, or allowed to run loose in the school from time to time. He will develop better with exercise providing it does not overtax him, or put any strain on his joints.

Chapter 5

Basic Foundation

At four years old the horse is ready to start more concentrated work. When riding him quietly on a contact, allow him to carry himself in a natural position with his head wherever he would like it (see plate 14). Try to encourage the horse to support himself, working as much as possible on his own. Ask him to go forward using one aid: both legs in contact, the inside leg actively in a vibrating movement on the girth, ie the upper part of the lower leg or calf is on the girth while the lower part and ankle are slightly behind. Ask very quietly and then wait for the response. If there is none, repeat the aid a little more clearly and then to help apply the whip directly behind your leg. Remember, the inside hind leg of the horse has to do more of the work and this is why we actively use our inside leg. We use it on the girth as the horse is thinner skinned in this area and therefore more sensitive.

When the horse goes forward it is not necessary to throw the reins away. On the other hand we definitely do not want to restrict the movement of his head or neck. The horse keeps his balance by the use of his head and neck in the same way that we use our arms. Allow the horse to take whatever contact he would like. If he goes on the forehand, be very careful not to support him with the hands, or let him use your hands as a fifth leg.

HAND CONTACT

Our aims at this point are that the horse should accept the leg and the hand, which of course he can only do if the rider is steady and in balance. The feeling of the rider's hand belongs in the horse's mouth and his hand and forearm should become part of the rein. He must let the horse take his hand. A horse will feel secure if he

Plate 14

knows where his rider's hand is; a little like a small child being led through a crowded store. The contact should be elastic. With a young horse that moves his head and neck a lot when he takes big strides forward, this is not always easy. To keep flexible contact with a following hand, you have to keep very relaxed in the wrist, elbow, and shoulder. I try to think of the elbow as being attached to the hip by a 2in piece of elastic so that the movement comes through the elbow and not straight to the shoulder. The hand should be passive – no fiddling with the fingers. The horse should not play with the bit but hold it quietly in his mouth without any grinding, chewing, or sideways jaw movement.

LEG CONTACT

The leg needs to stay in contact with the horse's side. This can only be done if the rider has a supple hip, knee and ankle. The rider needs to try and develop a 'feeling leg' so that he can be

Plate 15 Striking off a left lead canter with right hind down, K. Aftyka, Poland, on Kult

Plate 16 On the second beat of the canter, the inside hind and outside front strike together as a diagonal pair. Mrs J. Michael Plumb, USA, performing a medium canter on Midnight Cowboy

Plate 17 *A split second after the movement in plate 16, with the inside front just going to touch down. Richard Meade, UK, and The Wayfarer show the second beat in the canter with the horse now about to rock on to the inside front*

Plate 18 *M. Plewa and Virginia, Germany, demonstrate the third beat of a left lead canter with inside front down. A moment of suspension follows, then the same sequence, as shown in plates 15 on, begins again*

almost as sensitive with his leg as he is with his hands. With the horse accepting the leg and hand we have controlled forward movement.

Our next goal is to maintain an even rhythm in all paces. If the horse is naturally well balanced and carries himself in a horizontal position, he will probably keep a good rhythm. If the horse is not particularly well co-ordinated, the rider will need to think very much about keeping every stride the same. Some riders have no sense of rhythm and will need to develop this by singing, whistling or counting to themselves while they ride. Music also helps to keep the rider relaxed. The walk is a four beat pace with the legs being used in the sequence of inside hind, inside front, outside hind, outside front. When working in an arena, we assume that the side of the horse nearest to the wall is the outside and the other, the inside. Therefore, if moving in a clockwise direction or on the right rein, the right side of the horse is the inside. The trot is a two time pace with the legs being used in diagonal pairs. The horse should spring from one diagonal to the other and not push himself along as if he were on roller skates, or swing from one diagonal to the other like a camel. If the horse uses himself correctly in the trot, the rider should experience a pleasant round feeling. The canter is a three beat pace. The sequence of footfalls, if on the left rein are, right hind, left hind and right front together as a diagonal pair followed by the left front as the leading leg (see plates 15–18). When working on the right rein, the sequence would start with the left hind.

Once the horse maintains an even rhythm, he will become balanced and use himself more efficiently. The muscles over his loins and hind-quarters will develop and he will start to raise his head and neck a little if he was previously a little on his forehand (see figure 1, showing the change of the horse from the first year period to the second year period). The feeling of a more supple horse will become apparent when he starts to bend in the direction in which he is going. He will no longer fall in with the shoulder in the corners or on circles. The hind feet will follow in the tracks of the front feet and the hind-quarters will not swing out.

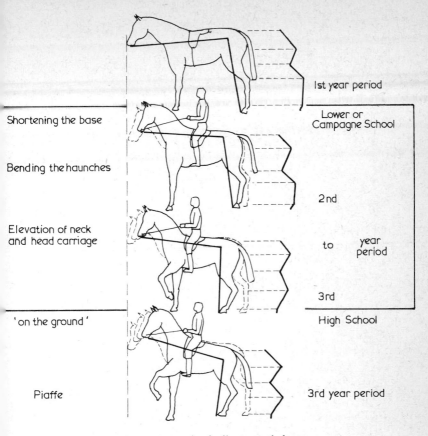

	1st year period
Shortening the base	Lower or Campagne School
Bending the haunches	2nd
Elevation of neck and head carriage	to year period
	3rd
'on the ground'	High School
Piaffe	3rd year period

Figure 1   Principle of collection and elevation

We now have our horse moving with controlled forward movement, in an even rhythm in all paces, and with the correct bend. Because he is in balance he will respond more willingly, as it will be relatively easy for him physically to perform all the simple school movements.

RISING TROT AND DIAGONALS

The horse has been worked mainly in the rising trot, and we use the outside diagonal, which means we rise as the outside front leg and the inside hind leg come forward and sit as they come to the ground. You can watch the outside shoulder, follow it forward and sit as it comes back. We use the outside diagonal to enable the inside hind leg to work more easily. It is easier for the rider to use the leg in the rising trot as he sits, which is when the inside hind is on the ground, thus activating it. He is up as the inside hind comes forward, which gives it more freedom to reach under. Once the horse starts responding to finer aids, the leg should be used whenever necessary, which could be on the up beat or at any time in the rising trot. A horse without a very generous nature soon learns that he can rest in between beats if the riders leg is applied in rhythm with the movement. When changing direction, change the diagonal by sitting for one beat of the trot. You must be careful when changing the diagonal, not to alter the angle of the upper body otherwise the horse's balance will be upset.

Before every aid is given, you must think exactly how you are going to execute it and exactly how you would like the horse to respond. This way you become very much aware of the horse's reactions. Remember how and when each aid was applied so that next time, if the response was desirable, you can do exactly the same. The horse will feel confident when he realises that his rider knows exactly what he is doing. Try not to anticipate the horse's reactions. In other words, if you ask him to trot, wait for him to go forward and go with him, do not get in front of the movement. You must be very much aware of the horse's every response and reaction. Now it is possible to set up a certain rapport with the horse; a partnership, with the horse wanting to work and please the rider. The rider should not have to demand and insist on every command but merely suggest to the horse with the horse in turn willingly responding. The aids should not be obvious to any bystander and the impression should be that everything is very easy. Dressage is an art, and spectators should never be given the picture of drive, push, and struggle.

SITTING TROT

As the horse becomes stronger, the rider can start to sit to the trot, being very much aware of any change in balance, position, or rhythm. If there is no change, then we know the horse is ready. If there is resistance, then the rider commences rising again and occasionally sits very lightly for just a few strides, going with the movement and thinking about maintaining exactly the same leg and hand contact. Invariably when the rider starts to sit, he stiffens and then loses contact, the horse then has cause to alter his balance and lose the rhythm. It is important to ensure that when going from rising to sitting trot, the angle of the upper body is not suddenly altered. Sometimes a good exercise for a rider or horse that stiffens is to change diagonals every three strides. The horse becomes used to frequent changes and it teaches the rider to remain in balance when he sits. For a horse that favours one diagonal, this is also a good exercise to encourage him to use both hind legs equally.

Once the horse has become accustomed to the rider in an upright, sitting position, work for only short periods of time. Frequent transitions, changes of direction, and large circles of 20m (66ft) at the sitting trot interspersed with periods of rising trot will keep the horse interested in his work. The transitions must always be forward with no loss of impulsion. At this stage, for a transition down, sit quietly, close the lower leg and become taller with the upper body, quietly stopping any back movement. The horse will go forward into the next pace without shortening his stride.

THE CANTER

We can now work on the canter. From a balanced sitting trot, as we come into the corner and as the horse starts to bend to the inside, we ask him to canter with a very definite and quick outside leg aid well back, at the same time taking the inside hip a little forward (see plate 19). The horse, remember, starts the canter with the outside hind and then drives with the inside hind, hence the aids. The rider must not lean forward or to the inside, as this gives the horse an additional problem to cope with. When the horse clearly understands the canter aids on both reins, work him

Plate 19   Miss Rachel Bayliss and Gurgle the Greek, UK, showing the canter aid

on a large circle. This will start to keep him in balance as he has to engage more from behind and will shorten his base from the back through to the front. If the horse should have a problem with one lead in the canter, then more work must be done in the trot to prepare him. The trot is the pace we work in mainly, the reason being that the horse has to use himself more evenly and it is easier to ask him to bend and then go straight.

RIDING CIRCLES

When the horse starts to work well and develops a good working trot (see plate 20) with impulsion, tracking up correctly, accepting the bit with his nose slightly in front of the vertical, we can make smaller circles 15m. When he can maintain his position and not lose impulsion on a 15m circle we can then make 10m (33ft)

Plate 20   Alison Oliver on HRH Princess Anne's Arthur of Troy in a working trot

*Plate 21   Beth Perkins, USA,
on Bally Cor*

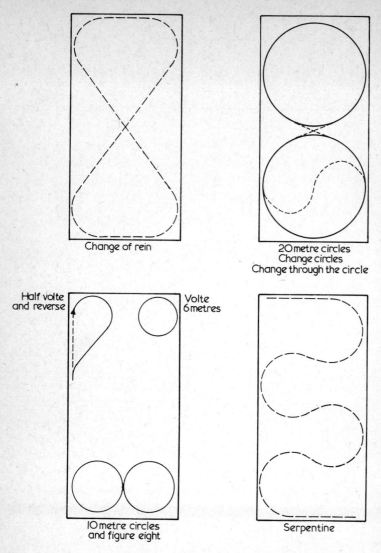

Figure 2 *School Movements*

circles. Before making any circle, make sure that the horse is listening to your inside leg. Use it a little before commencing the circle and then with both shoulders the same height, take the outside shoulder forward, and look in the direction of the circle. The horse should come from your inside leg into the outside rein. The inside rein can be very slightly open. Some riders can maintain a better position by thinking 'inside shoulder back' as they commence a circle (see plate 21).

When riding in an arena with a young horse, we make the corners round, only going into them on the bend that we have on a 15m and later a 10m circle. If we go into the corner too deeply and the horse is not yet sufficiently supple to make a turn, the hind-quarters will swing out. We should not have to actively hold the hind-quarters with the outside leg back. If the horse is correctly working with the inside hind, the quarters will not swing out. Only if we ask too much of him and so cause a problem will this happen, and it could not be classified as an evasion. To differentiate between what is a physical problem and what is an evasion, takes experience and a keen understanding of your horse.

So far, we have worked mainly in an enclosed area or at least on a flat area, The horse should also be hacked out frequently and allowed to go on a long rein and balance himself. Use any hills and uneven ground to help him adjust to changes of terrain. If you come to a flat area work for a few minutes on large circles and changes of rein. The greater variety of areas you can work in, the less likely the horse is of becoming bored. Even when out in the open, try and be thinking ahead all the time of how and where you would like the horse to go. In a field, pick a tree, post, or bunch of thistles and see if you can ride straight towards it. Ride circles by starting with the idea of the exact size you intend to make them. Again, start and finish at a chosen spot. A circle can only be round, not pear, egg or any other shape.

If you have problems with geometry, practice drawing the school movements and then ride them in your mind (see figure 2 showing school movements). Some people need to put a track of lime or sawdust down so that they can aquire a good idea of circles and the different sizes.

Chapter 6

Cavalletti

Cavalletti, used for exercises to make a horse supple, are useful whether it is being trained as a jumper, hunter, event or dressage horse. When working over the poles, the horse has to spring gymnastically from one diagonal to the other using all the joints of his hind legs and rounding his back.

The first exercise is to walk the horse quietly over a single pole on the ground. Once he is doing this calmly, put six to eight poles on the ground at 4ft intervals, if possible next to a wall or a fence line. With this number of poles, the horse is less likely to try and jump over the whole lot. Walk over the poles from both directions, first taking him in the direction he prefers. Shorten the stirrup leathers a hole or two, so that there is more bend in the knee and the angle between the thigh and the lower leg is decreased. This will make it easier to go with the movement of the horse.

Work the horse in the trot until he is going calmly and then in rising trot, ride over the poles. If he is inclined to rush, work him on a circle in front of the cavalletti and when he has settled, quietly approach them again. Allow the horse to put his head down only if he wishes, by throwing the reins away you will not *make* him do so. Trotting poles may be used several times a week without harming the horse in any way. As time goes on, the poles can be gradually raised, up to 6in – 1ft so that the horse has to bend even more and approaches a collected trot position (see plate 22).

Once the horse is really using himself and going straight without evading in any way, intervals between the cavalletti can be enlarged. Gradually, a few inches at a time, we can work on lengthening the stride, by moving the poles from 4ft up to 6ft apart depending on the horse. After creating sufficient impulsion

Plate 22

by asking the horse to really bend and work from behind, we can now work him in an extended trot for a few strides without him rushing or dropping on his forehand.

CANTERING CAVALLETTI

We can also help the horse in his canter by using the cavalletti. Putting them at their lowest height and spaced at 9ft intervals, we can bring the horse trotting through. He would have to be on a 4ft 6in stride so as not to run into difficulties by thinking that he should try to trot a pole at a time. Canter the horse quietly on a circle and then without altering in any way, come quietly down over the cavalletti. Again, make sure to work from both directions and always finish on a good note. The cavalletti may be raised gradually up to a height of 18in. With the poles 9ft apart, the horse now has to bounce and come through from behind much quicker. If the horse has a problem with lengthening his stride, lower the cavalletti and lengthen them gradually out to 12ft apart.

There are many different combinations you can use for trotting poles, such as staggering them at odd distances. This makes the horse think and adjust from a short to a longer stride very easily. They may also be used on a 15m or larger circle. The horse can be taken from the inside of the circle, which will be a short stride, gradually to the outside where the stride will be long. This is a very difficult exercise and should only be done by a horse at a more advanced level and with an experienced rider.

When the horse is going quietly forward over trotting poles at 4ft 6in apart, place a cantering cavalletti 9ft past the last pole. The horse now will come trotting through and take one stride after the last pole and canter over the 18in cavalletti. We can build this up gradually to 2ft 6in and 3ft high, later making it wider and into parallel rails. This will teach the horse to jump in good style and really round himself over a fence.

If you have a horse that has difficulty taking one particular lead in the canter, work on a circle trotting over a single cavalletti. As he takes the correct lead over the cavalletti, keep him cantering for a short while.

Although the use of cavalletti is not absolutely necessary for the dressage horse and it is not used in the classical school, it will not create any problems. In fact the requirement of a small jump after a dressage test is asked in some countries. As trends change to a certain degree with all art forms it is wise to keep an open mind and a broad outlook. On the whole, cavalletti is a valuable exercise especially for the timid rider and will accustom him to a more active movement of the horse. It will instill in him more confidence in himself should the horse unfortunately stumble, shy, or even buck.

Chapter 7

Second Stage of Training

SHOULDER-IN

When you feel that the horse is maintaining a good rhythm in the trot and engaging well behind on a 10m circle, start thinking about the shoulder-in. This is a good exercise for making the horse supple. He is bent away from the direction in which he is travelling. The only other time this happens is in the counter canter. The shoulder-in should be performed in the collected trot and the important points to watch are that the horse is only slightly bent to the inside and that the inner hind leg is supporting more weight (see plates 23–24). For the rider who has not had the opportunity to sit on a horse that already does shoulder-in, it may be to their advantage to start at the walk. Care must be taken, however, not to do too much in the walk in case it becomes unnecessarily shortened.

As you come out of the corner to start on the long side of the circle, maintain the bend as though you were intending to change the rein across on the diagonal ie the inside leg is actively on the girth with the outside leg supporting behind the girth. The outside shoulder is slightly forward with both hands slightly in the direction of the inside. Remember it is shoulder-in and not head to the inside. If you think of your inside hand as the horse's inside shoulder and your outside hand as his outside shoulder, it will help. As you come around the corner, the horse's shoulders must come to the inside and not go straight on down the track. The hind-quarters should stay on the track. In the beginning stages, bring the shoulder to the inside very slightly so that the shoulder-in is very shallow. Don't be frightened to make the movement of your outside shoulder coming forward very definite. The horse,

49

Plates 23/24 The author performing shoulder-ins

if in the correct position, will again be going from your inside leg on the girth, and into the outside rein. If you can give the inside rein and the horse stays in shoulder-in, then it will be correct. Do not bring your inside leg back and push the quarters out as this is not shoulder-in but displacement of the quarters. Also, make sure that when you use the inside leg, you don't drop the inside shoulder. Both shoulders must be the same height. Once you can feel the shoulder-in in the walk for a few steps, proceed in sitting trot. If the first few steps are adequate, you can come from the shoulder-in onto a circle. Later, when you can get halfway down the arena, or about 20m (66ft) with the horse maintaining the rhythm and not stiffening, proceed back onto the track and ride straight on. If the horse becomes inactive, a tap with the whip just after the inside leg has been used will correct him. If as is the normal tendency with most riders, you find that you are using either too much or an indirect inside rein, then simply let it go for a stride or two. Be aware immediately of how the horse responds. It is his reward after you have asked him, to allow him to perform the movement. Reward him again verbally or with a pat.

Gradually, as the horse responds, we can ask for a little more angle. As the horse becomes more supple, he can increase the angle, offering no resistance and moving on four tracks. As the inside hind comes more underneath him supporting more weight, the forehand is made free so that the inside shoulder can move well forward, with the inside leg crossing over in front of the outside leg. Thus, the horse becomes more collected. The horse should perform the shoulder-in, equally on both reins.

MEDIUM TROT

In the medium trot the horse should lengthen his frame with increased impulsion, and quicken the tempo to almost that of a 'roads and tracks' trot. The medium trot is not just an ordinary trot but means that the gait should become big, strong and more expressive.

Plate 25   The author doing a medium trot on Star Task

From the shoulder-in, we can start working towards a medium trot (see plate 25). Make a few strides of shoulder-in and then go across on the diagonal, asking for a longer stride or medium trot. The horse will probably go quite willingly forward and really reach out. The rider must make sure he allows the horse to lengthen his whole frame and stretch his neck out, but not down. Before reaching the track on the other side of the arena, or if you are working outside, at a given point, make a definite transition back to a working trot. Sit down, close the legs maintaining impulsion and keeping the rhythm and a little taller with the upper body so he comes into a receiving hand, and you will get a forward smooth transition. Try now coming across on the diagonal and at X ask for a longer stride and again make a transition back before the corner. When hacking out, make use of any gentle slopes, asking the horse for a longer more active trot. As he starts up the slope, ask for more impulsion. He can not drop down and if you go forward with him, it will come very easily.

THE EXTENDED TROT

The extension will come gradually and if you acquire a few strides, be happy, do not ask for more. One of the biggest faults that occurs in training is to expect too much too soon. You must feel when the horse is ready to perform a new exercise and tell from his immediate response whether you were correct in your judgements. If there is no resistance and the horse understands, you will know you were correct. If he does resist, you must assess whether he is physically unprepared or mentally needs to be presented with the exercise in a different manner, eg some horses will come into a shoulder-in better from a circle than from a corner.

The rider must make sure in the extended trot, that he does not push the horse too much and cause an unevenness of stride. The extensions can be done in rising trot in the beginning and as the horse progresses, in sitting trot. If the horse uses himself correctly, the trot should not be difficult to sit to (see plate 26). If, however, he hollows his back or gets an exaggerated movement, waving his forelegs out in front, he may be uncomfortable.

THE ORDINARY CANTER

When the horse is performing consistently in the trot, we work on the canter. Thinking very definitely of a three beat movement or humming your favourite waltz tune work on large circles to encourage the horse to shorten his stride. You must make sure that you sit very still in the canter, without swinging the upper body or sliding the seat bones – and no boat rowing movements with the hands. Just sit and allow your hips to go with the movement, keeping still with the upper body (see plate 27). To sit still of course, means to make no unnecessary or involuntary movement. It will be helpful to think of a round soft canter as though the horse were going very slightly up hill. It is very easy, if the horse is on his forehand, to fall forward with the upper body thus pushing him even more down hill. At the moment in the canter when the horse feels up in front of you, he may need to be steadied with a half halt.

Plate 26   John Winnett, USA, sitting to the extended trot

THE HALF HALT

The half halt is very frequently misinterpreted. It is not as a lot of riders think, half of a halt; a long slow drawn out whoa, similar to the stopping of a stage coach. It is when the horse is brought to attention for only a moment; a moment of collection. All the rider needs to do is to correct his position, or carry himself more elegantly for a moment, by sitting tall and relaxing the seat thus allowing the horse to come up to his seat bones and fill out between his legs. When the horse feels the rider carrying himself, he will usually respond immediately by picking himself up a little. If a rider has a sloppy upper body, he may need to think of pushing his stomach forward or to relax and drop the seat a little heavier with closed legs. If the horse is very active you may need only a little vibration with the inside rein which will steady the movement through to the inside hind leg. Should the horse tend to be on the forehand you may need a definite hip forward movement with a lifting of the upper body and a little pressure of both legs and a momentary restraining hand.

Plate 27   An ordinary canter demonstrated by M. Plewa and Virginia

The co-ordination and timing of these aids is important for an effective result.

You should feel that the horse becomes rounder and a little elevated. A common fault is when the rider tries to 'drive the hind legs under the horse' and instead causes the horse to hollow and stiffen his back. The half halt must come through the whole horse from behind in a continuous and round backed movement.

Plate 28   Captain Mark Phillips, UK, on Columbus

Plate 29   Sidley Payne, USA, on her American Quarter Horse, Scarteen

The main point to remember is that the half halt is a forward movement and should not be obvious to the bystander.

THE COLLECTED AND EXTENDED CANTER

The moment the horse is carrying himself in a horizontal position, we can ask him to engage more from behind and gradually become more collected in his canter (see plates 28–29). As soon as he has developed an even and regular collected canter, then we work on extending or gradually lengthening the stride as we did in the trot (see plate 30). Come from a circle or the short wall of the arena and ask for more impulsion, allowing the horse to stretch out, lengthening his whole frame.

For transitions down from the canter, it is often advisable to come onto a circle and then ask, so that the horse does not go into the trot with long strides. After the canter, you will find that the trot invariably becomes more beautiful. The canter gives much more impulsion and creates a very active trot (see plate 31).

THE WALK

When the horse has been really working well, we give him frequent periods of walk, at first on a contact in ordinary walk (see plate 32) and then at the free walk on a long rein (see plate 33). If he has been working well and using his back, he will want to stretch out and at the same time take a longer stride, over tracking by at least 8in. The contact in the free walk should be only the weight of the rein so that one can keep the horse going straight.

By working mostly in the trot the canter is improved, which in turn improves the walk. In the walk, we ride the horse on a contact and allow him to go forward but are very careful not to over-ride him as any stiffness or unevenness will be very apparent. In plate 34 the horse is in a collected walk. If the horse is not correctly bending all the joints of the hind legs or has a stiff back he will not always correctly accept the bit. All stiffness and resistance is shown or felt in the horse's mouth. He may for example be heavy in the hand, but this does not mean that he has a hard mouth. He probably is not using himself actively behind or carrying himself. On the other hand he can be light on the bit, but with no mouth because he has no movement from behind, or because the rider will not ride on a contact.

No hands are not good hands. Good hands are those that do not interfere with the horse's movement or cause a resistance and can only come from an independent seat.

Plate 30 Mary Gordon Watson, UK, and The Cornishman

Plate 31 Edwin Brysor and Thunder, Ireland

Plate 32   Sue Hatherly, UK, rides Devil's Jump in an ordinary walk

Plate 33   Another Folly, ridden by Major Jeremy Beale, UK, in a free walk

Plate 34   HRH the Princess Anne on Goodwill

THE HALT

The horse should halt squarely and so be in a position to move forward immediately without having to gather himself together (see plate 35). Halt by a wall or fence and try to feel whether the halt is square. You may have to check by looking and then associate what you see with what you feel. The same applies for diagonals in the trot and the leads in the canter. If a hind leg is back, use the leg on the girth on the same side. If a front leg is back, use the leg a little forward.

TURN ON THE HAUNCHES

When turning from the halt or walk, the horse will turn most easily on the centre. That is, moving both the front and hind legs, pivoting from his middle. The turn on the forehand is used by some trainers, but is generally considered to be an unnatural movement. For a rider who needs to develop his feel with the legs, this exercise may be useful. It does very little for most horses as we are trying most of our time to get them off their forehands. Once the horse has learnt to swing his quarters away from the leg, we will be inclined to have problems when correcting the horse in the halt. Instead of bringing his hind legs forward, he will swing them away. I like to think that the leg asks the horse to go forward or to be more active. Once he learns evasions, we have to spend all our time keeping the hind-quarters straight. It starts to end up like a rhumba with the rider doing too much and eventually carrying the horse, instead of the horse carrying himself with the rider giving the directions.

As we are mainly concerned with the control of the hind-quarters, we concentrate on the turn on the haunches or pirouette as it is called when performed from the walk or the canter (see plate 36). If a rider is not completely confident in his application of the aids when teaching the horse to make a turn on the haunches, it is advisable to start from the halt. From a square halt the horse should pivot on the inside hind leg, picking his feet

Plate 35 Mary Gordon Watson and The Cornishman
demonstrate a square halt

Plate 36   A pirouette

up in the rhythm of the walk and bending in the direction he is going (see plate 37). The hind feet describe a small half circle while the front feet describe a much larger half circle with the outside front leg crossing over in front of the inside front leg. Make the first turn in the direction in which the horse bends most easily.

The turn on the haunches is a forward movement, therefore, our first aid is to ask the horse with the inside leg to go forward. As he is about to move, we look to the inside, moving the outside shoulder forward with the hands slightly to the inside. Care must be taken that the contact is even and not stronger with the inside rein, thus bending the horse's neck too much. As the

Plate 37   Correct positioning for a turn on the haunches with the horse coming forward from the rider's inside leg

horse starts to move to the inside, let your outside leg slide well back behind the girth to keep the hind legs in position. The horse should now move forwards and sideways with his forehand. When the half turn of 180° has been completed, walk straight forward by reversing the aids, as the opposite leg will now be on the inside. The rider must be careful not to lean back, as although the horse needs to be on his haunches it is a forward movement. When the horse performs this exercise well, try

Plate 38   The author reigning back Madeira

coming from the walk; almost halt, keeping the horse moving from behind and ask for the turn, keeping the bend to the inside, but controlling it with the outside hand and maintaining the walk. If you have problems, take one step at a time with a pause in between steps, or one step and then walk forward. Hopefully these corrections will probably only be needed once or twice.

THE REIN BACK

The rein back may be used only when the horse is going forward and has reached a reasonable degree of suppleness. From a square halt, the horse steps back, using his legs in diagonal pairs with his back round and the hind legs well under him (see plate 38). The horse should stay in a round position and step back keeping straight. We always teach him alongside a wall or fence-line to help control the quarters. The rider should ask the horse to go forward with his inside leg on the girth, and as the horse starts forward into his receiving and passively resisting hand, he should use very quiet alternate rein aids, taking and giving quietly, each step. If the horse comes back one or two steps, allow him to walk straight forward on a contact. The rider must always know exactly how many steps back he intends his horse to take as it is very easy to have the horse coming back more than you would like. If the horse should be inclined to swing his quarters in because he does not want to round his back and bend the joints in his hind legs, the rider should use his inside leg back a little. Usually, only four to six steps should be asked and the horse then allowed to go forward into the walk, trot, and later the canter.

In the rein back, the rider may need to sit light and even lean a shade forward to allow the horse full use of his back. On no account should the rider lean back and pull as this will only make the horse run back with his head up and a hollow back, through fear of the discomfort or pain in his mouth. This would defeat the purpose of the exercise. The horse should not drag his feet back and should not weave from one diagonal to the other. These are indications of stiffness.

We can now combine some of our exercises and come from the turn on the haunches into the canter, rein back and into trot or canter, and shoulder-in and into extended trot, thus making work more varied and interesting. We practise all the school movements as in figures 2–3, making sure that we realise the purpose of these movements. If the horse is going straight, he must be straight. If the horse is a little stiff with the hind-quarters coming in, we work in shoulder-fore or position the forehand slightly to the inside. By correcting this way, rather than by pushing the quarters back we encourage the horse to bend and take more weight on the inside hind leg.

HAUNCHES-IN OR TRAVERSE

The haunches-in is asked for only when the horse is performing a good shoulder-in. The horse will come down the long side of the arena looking in the direction that he is going, ie bent to the inside with his forehand on the track and the hind-quarters

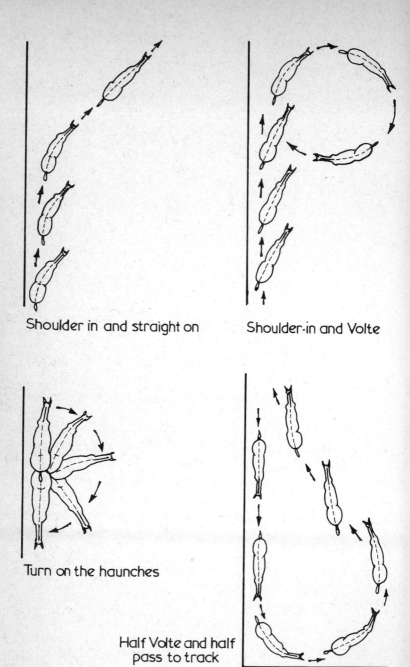

Shoulder in and straight on

Shoulder-in and Volte

Turn on the haunches

Half Volte and half
pass to track

Figure 3   Second stage school movements

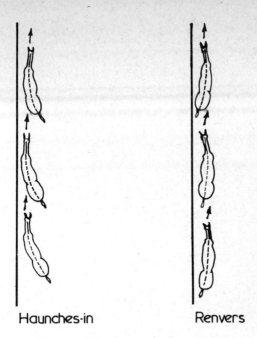

Haunches-in   Renvers

Figure 4 Second stage school movements

slightly to the inside (see figure 4). Ask for only a slight displacement of the quarters coming from the corner with the outside hip and leg back. You should feel that you are sitting on the inside of the track and not leaning towards the outside leg. Concentrate on keeping the rhythm and forward movement with the inside leg on the girth. The inside hand by the wither should control the bend (see plate 39).

A good exercise is that of shoulder-in, straight for a few strides and then haunches-in alternating every few strides. If the horse is correctly bent and accepting the inside leg you will have no problem of the horse using the haunches-in to evade engaging correctly with the inside hind.

HALF PASS

The horse should now be ready to start work on two tracks or half pass (see diagram 3). Bring him in collected trot (see plate 40) and make a half circle in the corner onto the centre line. Maintain

69

Plate 39   Mrs Plumb demonstrates a travers or haunches in

the bend by putting the horse in a shoulder-in position, at the
same time sliding the outside leg back, not too quickly or he
will confuse it with the canter aid. Keep your shoulders at
the same height and parallel with the short wall or at a right

Plate 40 Bruce Davidson and Irish Cap, USA, going into a half pass from a collected trot

angle to the long wall. The inside hand is by the wither maintaining the slight bend to the inside, while the inside leg is on the girth. The horse will come forwards and then sideways.

The horse should always look slightly in the direction he is going with the forehand slightly to the inside (see plate 41). Think of keeping the rhythm and of the horse going forwards and then sideways. As the horse becomes increasingly supple, he will cross over more with the outside front leg. You must feel as though the outside seat bone is going in the direction of your inside hand. That is, if making a half pass to the left, the left hand controls the bend and prevents the forehand from dropping over to the left. The left leg is on the girth for forward movement, with the outside or right leg and hip back to keep the hind-quarters moving over. You must make sure that you do not drop the right shoulder or collapse the right hip. When the horse arrives at the track by the quarter marker, or chosen spot if working outside, you must change your aids and prepare for the corner.

When the horse moves on two tracks on both reins and does the movements, 'down the centre and two track to the track', and 'half volte and two track to the halfway mark' we can come from the quarter marker to X and back to the next quarter marker. Later we can do zig-zag two tracks down the centre line. It may be helpful to refer to figure 5 showing the arena with halfway and quarter markers.

RENVERS

Renvers is performed on the long wall in collected trot with the hind-quarters on the track, the forehand in, and with the horse looking in the direction that he is going, ie opposite to shoulder-in (see figure 4).

Start the movement from the corner with the horse maintaining the bend as though he were to change the rein. As the forehand comes off the track, change the bend and position to the outside so that your outside leg is on the girth maintaining the bend and

Plate 41   The author on Goldlack in a half-pass

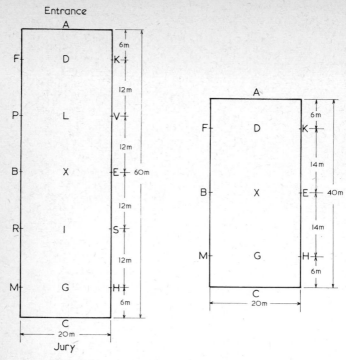

Public to be at least 20m (66ft) from all sides of arena

Figure 5   Dressage arenas

forward movement while your inside leg and hip come back behind the girth keeping the hind-quarters on the track.

COUNTER CANTER

Before we start working on the counter canter we need to make sure that the horse is straight in the canter. Most horses tend to carry the hind-quarters to the inside and therefore do not work correctly from behind. We straighten the horse by using a very slight shoulder-in and later renvers.

When the horse can maintain his impulsion in the canter on a 10m circle, we think about working in counter canter. Counter canter helps to prepare the horse for flying changes and keeps him supple. Make a half circle to the centre line and change the

Plate 42 Mn. Fouzaint, France, in a counter canter. Compare with plate 17, the same moment exactly, but leading off different legs

rein, back to the halfway marker. You must now stay on the outside lead with the horse slightly bent to the outside (see plate 42). You need not go too deep into the corners but must maintain your position, thinking of the rhythm all the time. Remember, if you can be quick with the aids then you can be light. If an aid is applied almost before there is a problem, very little needs to be done. If it is late, then invariably you have to do more. The whole idea is based on timing and this is why the rhythm is so important.

SIMPLE CHANGES AND THE FLYING CHANGE

Once the horse can make 20m circles and serpentines of 15m loops, we can think about flying changes. We would also by this time have worked on 'walk to canter' and 'canter to walk' and made simple changes. In the beginning, our simple changes would have been performed by making two or three trot strides and then changing the lead. The simple change is made on the diagonal or the imaginary line between the quarter markers. It can be done at X or just before the corner.

When working on the flying change, it is best to take the horse on the lead which he prefers least. Make a half circle and reverse to the halfway. Counter canter along the long side and as you come to the quarter marker before the corner, change the leg aids clearly, bringing the outside leg back. The bend of course, is changed for the corner. The horse should jump through and take a full canter stride onto the true lead. Care must be taken not to swing the upper body or shift your weight. The horse will usually change onto his easier lead readily and then we can try in the other direction. Once he has accomplished the changes we can make a serpentine and change on the centre line with every change of direction. We can of course, change at X but it is wise to do it at the quarter markers and then on the long sides of the arena.

The changes should be straight, without the horse swinging from one side to the other. The rider likewise should move as little as possible. Keep working in counter canter so that the horse does not anticipate a change. He must wait for the aids and not make them on his own accord.

When the horse is very obedient in his changes, you can think about performing them on the long sides, changing every six strides and then five, four and three. Make sure you know exactly how many strides you intend the horse to take before making a change. It may take many months before you progress to three tempo changes. When the horse is correct on the long side, we work on the diagonal.

As with all new exercises, care must be taken not to apply too strong an aid. Trust the horse by asking quietly, but very positively and waiting for and letting the result happen.

THE PIROUETTE

The pirouette is performed from a collected canter (see plate 36, page 64). Start by coming down the long wall a good horse's length off the track in renvers. As you approach the short wall, ask the horse for a very small three-quarter circle towards the corner and proceed on the short wall. Gradually decrease the size of the circle making sure to maintain a correct three beat canter. It can also be started from a half pass and then eventually when going in a straight line. The hind-quarters need to be well under control, keeping the bend to the inside. With the inside leg actively on the girth and outside leg back, the outside hip back and both shoulders the same height with the outside one a little forward, make a half halt. The horse should make three to four strides in a half pirouette of 180°, four to six strides in a three-quarter pirouette of 270° and six to eight strides in a full pirouette of 360°. The hind legs must not be fixed but must keep the canter rhythm. If the horse should start to lose impulsion in the pirouette, take him out of it by riding straight forward.

Chapter 8

Arena Technique

During the course of training, you may wish to compete in a dressage competition. It is helpful to see how the horse reacts under different conditions and to have the judges' opinion of your performance. You can also evaluate your standards by watching the other competitors and by the results of the competition.

Make sure that you read all the conditions of the show and whatever rules that apply to the tests you decide to ride, beforehand. For example, which bits are allowed, the attire which is accepted, and whether spurs are mandatory. It is a good idea to accustom the horse to the use of spurs (see plate 43) by wearing them beforehand. They are a finer aid and should be used only in advanced training. The double bridle will also have been used if necessary, riding at first mainly on the bridoon or snaffle (see plate 44).

Before your first competition, it is helpful to have a dry run or rehearsal. Plait or braid the horse to make sure that he does not object to a different hair-do. Load him in a trailer and drive to the home of a friend preferably where there is an arena of the size that you will be competing in. The small arena is 20m by 40m (66ft x 132ft), the large arena 20m by 60m (66ft x 198ft) (see figure 5, page 74). The markers will always be in the same places. Only the large arena will have the additional markers, VSRPLI. You should work the horse in for the length of time that it usually requires for him to start to concentrate, also giving him enough time to physically loosen up. You should have a friend call the test for you while you ride it through, also timing it to make sure that you are within the time limit. Make sure that the horse is used to the salute. Ladies drop their right hand behind their thigh and bow the head to the judges in a positive movement,

Plate 43

Plate 44

gentlemen take the hat off with their right hand and with the opening to the back, drop the hat also behind the thigh. (The impression that the judges are given if the hat has the opening to the front is that the rider requires a donation.) In the salute, a smile

Plate 45 Beth Perkins working in her horse without stirrups to keep a relaxed thigh and a deep seat

gives the impression that you enjoy competing and it helps to relieve any tension. If you need to repeat any movements, do so, but it is wise not to ride through the test too many times. Some horses learn very quickly when they are on show and anticipate the commands.

WORKING IN

If you go to the show with the attitude that it is for the further education of the horse and not to win a prize, you will be more relaxed and therefore more likely to show the horse at his best. You should by now have an idea of the required length of time it takes to work your horse in (see plate 45). If their riders are inclined to be nervous, some horses will tend to do better if they are lunged for 20-30 minutes. This will mean that at least one party is calm when the competition begins. Another horse will need very little working in, maybe a walk on a long rein for 10 minutes and a short trot and canter with frequent transitions. Some horses go well after a long trailer ride; some go well if they have not eaten and some if they have a full belly. It may take a few shows to find out exactly which method to adopt for your horse. Ideally, it is best to take as short a period as possible to prepare but long enough to loosen up both horse and rider.

Another preparation for competitions is to make sure that your horse is used to working in wind, heat, cold and rain; that he is also used to different footing such as turf, sand, mud and hard earth. Naturally he will have his preferences, but he must be able to perform whatever the conditions.

DRESS

Dress conservatively, in the traditional manner. For the lower levels, a hacking jacket with a shirt and tie, a hunting-cap, breeches and boots are suitable at small shows. At the larger shows, light buff, canary- or stone-coloured breeches with gloves to match, white stock or white shirt with a dark tie, black boots, black jacket and a bowler or hunting-cap are worn. For the higher levels such as the Prix St George and above, white breeches, stock, cutaway or tail-coat with a top hat, white gloves and spurs are required (see plate 46). You should not wear white gloves unless you have to. Only if the horse is exceptionally steady and you have inconspicuously quiet hands will you get away without a comment on 'obvious aids' from the judge.

Hopefully, the competition will be well organised and you will have the exact time you are expected to enter the arena. As soon as the rider preceding you leaves the arena, you should ride around the outside as close as you can to the markers, flower-pots, shrubs and judges' stand. Make sure that the horse is going well, as although he is not being marked yet, the judge is being given his first impression. It would be helpful if he could be thinking, 'This one looks promising'. If your horse has any problems of shying, try to keep calm and take your time. If he is not going forward, do not be afraid to make him move on around the outside.

When the bell rings, the rider should come to the entrance of the arena and make a small circle in the direction the horse bends less easily and then drop his whip. A rider will be eliminated for carrying a whip into the arena. As the horse comes down the centre line, he will be straight. The rider should fix his eyes on the judges and ride forward in a good active trot. Remember, it is the horse which is being judged, not the rider. If the horse comes off the centre line it is better to leave him where he is as you will end up with a snake-like movement if you are not very careful. Try to look confident as though to say 'here I am, the one you have been waiting for!'

When halting, make a square halt, with the X under the horse's belly. If the halt is not square, correct it, but if you feel that the horse may step back or sideways, leave it as it is. After the smart but not flowery salute, proceed straight forward, try to relax and *do* keep breathing.

If possible, have the test read by someone with a clear and soothing voice. The reader should stand by the B or the E marker and

Plate 46 John Winnett on Reinold performing in top class competition

keep just one movement ahead of the one being performed by
the rider. Each movement may only be read once and must be
called as written on the test sheet. You will of course have learnt
the test by either walking it on foot in the arena or by drawing the
pattern of the test on paper.

Do not be surprised if the horse does something he has never done before. It often happens and should not upset you. If, for example, he takes a wrong lead, quietly come back to the trot and ask again. Remember, do not use your voice as this is penalised. Generally, by the time you have ridden halfway through the test, things start to flow more as both horse and rider begin to relax. Remember the golden rule for the correction of all problems, *ride your horse forward*, and look in the direction of your next movement.

After the final salute, leave the arena in an active free walk. The test has not ended until the rider passes through the gateway. Leave the arena in a dignified manner and reward the horse, giving him a pleasant memory of the arena.

It is wise to try and ride two or three tests if possible. You will know afterwards exactly what you need to work on for the next test. If you become very nervous, sit down somewhere quiet and collapse for a while. Think positively that everything will be calm, quiet and exactly as you would like with no effort. About 80 per cent of riding depends on the rider's mental attitude.

Chapter 9

Judging

It is very useful, if you are interested in dressage competitions, to know what the judge is looking for. In the different levels or stages of training, emphasis is put more on certain movements and how they are performed, than on others. In all levels, the most important points are that the horse should have pure gaits; a four beat walk, a two beat trot, a three beat canter and a two beat rein back, all with even rhythms. The horse should be calm, active, supple, light and obedient.

At the novice level, the judge will expect the horse to be going on a contact, quietly accepting the leg and hand. The horse should be working in the trot with sufficient energy so that he carries himself. If the horse is on a loose rein, it does not necessarily mean that he is light. One expects lightness more at an advanced stage, when the horse is collected and carries himself lightly. The rhythm should be maintained especially in corners and on circles. The horse will not be expected to go into the corners at this stage but should make nice round ones, bending very slightly to the inside.

The judge will not be too harsh if the transitions are not exactly at the marker, as long as they are forward and smooth. You should try to be as accurate as possible but not at the expense of a rough transition, which may be inclined to upset the horse for the rest of the test. If something goes wrong and it is quietly corrected, the judge will also be fairly lenient. A transition is considered correct if performed when the rider's shoulder is opposite the marker. The judge will be more concerned with the over-all picture than with individual movements. The horse should look happy and free in his movement. The judge may mark a rider down a little if a circle is not round but is egg, pear, orange, or plum shaped. If it is obviously clear that the rider is not thinking sufficiently ahead

Plate 47 Demonstrating a collected canter in a test

or cuts the corners and starts on the change across the diagonal too soon, missing the marker on the next long side, the judge may be more harsh.

Remember, each movement in the test sometimes consists of several exercises. If the main part of the movement is excellent and the rest is adequate, you will probably only obtain a 'sufficient' or slightly higher mark. For each movement there is a mark and the judge will also make a brief comment of appreciation, encouragement or some constructive criticism.

The judge will have a preconceived idea of the standard he expects from each level and will mark accordingly. He will also mark your test as he sees it executed. Previous tests should mean nothing to him – but human nature is difficult to change. If you perform much better in the second test, you are likely to obtain proportionately much higher marks from an understanding judge.

Plate 48 The author and Star Task in the dressage phase of a Three-Day-Event

SCORING

Each movement is marked out of ten and if you score five or better you should be satisfied for your first test. The 'General Impressions' at the end of the test are most important. If you have three good paces which are regular and even, you should get a seven or an eight. If the horse has two very good paces and one bad, you can only expect an 'insufficient' or a four. The impulsion should be sufficient to obtain a good working trot. The impulsion required is not just looked upon as forward movement, but the elasticity of the forward movement.

If the horse with good paces makes quiet, calm transitions with no resistances and bends a little without hanging on the bit, he should be marked with seven or an eight.

In the novice level the judge will expect the rider to be sitting in a good working position. The aids should not be obvious. If the aids used produce the required effect, the judge should accept them. If they are obviously ineffective, he may comment. There are many roads that lead to Rome and although the judge may not agree with your method of training, he should appreciate the results.

As the tests become increasingly more difficult, the judge will expect the same correctness but more precision. The trot becomes more collected and should be appreciated for the slightest elevation. Only later will it become cadenced or show more expression and brilliance. The shoulder-in, extensions, or any new requirements will not be expected to be shown to perfection.

At each stage, the horse will be expected to carry himself in a certain frame. This of course will vary, depending on how the horse carries himself naturally. If the young horse is well balanced and naturally carries himself well, the judge should not mark him down for moving in a more advanced frame. It may be difficult for the judge to know how the horse moves and carries himself at liberty, but the rider will know. As the horse comes to the advanced levels, he will be expected to perform very accurately but not at the expense of any freedom or brilliance.

The judge may, if he has time, give the rider a brief critique at the end of the test. This will actually save him time as it does not have to be dictated to a secretary or writer. It will of course also help the rider as he will have fresh in his mind, exactly how the test rode. The judge should give helpful comments on how to improve the performance and what needs to be concentrated on for the further development of the horse.

Hopefully, the judge will remember his first time in a dressage competition and be sympathetic to novice riders. If they are not sitting in a very elegant position, he should try to give one or two simple suggestions on how to improve their posture. You should be able to ride in competition and enjoy the experience of being appreciated and at the same time accept any constructive criticism. You should not compete for the reason of being told how good you are. This applies to lessons as well. If you want to learn, you must accept corrections.

Remember, the judge can only comment on what he sees during the test. You may not give an accurate presentation of the true capabilities of either the horse or yourself. This you must know, and be content only in your own mind if you have performed as best you can and in a sporting manner.

Index